Praises, Prayers, and Petitions

Adoration before the Blessed Sacrament

by
Keith Wayne Phillips

*All booklets are published thanks to the
generous support of the members of the
Catholic Truth Society*

CATHOLIC TRUTH SOCIETY
PUBLISHERS TO THE HOLY SEE

Contents

Preface 3

Adoration 6

Belief 8

Calling 10

Deeds 12

Eternity. 14

Faith 16

Grace 18

Holiness 20

Idolatry. 22

Joy 24

Kindness. 26

Love 28

Mercy 30

Need 32

Openness 34

Peace 36

Quietness 38

Respect. 40

Salvation. 42

Trust 44

Unity 46

Vanity 48

Worldliness. 49

X=Christ. 51

Yearning 53

Zeal 55

ISBN 978 1 86082 876 8

PREFACE

"In the liturgy of the Mass we express our faith in the real presence of Christ under the species of bread and wine by, among other ways, genuflecting or bowing deeply as a sign of adoration of the Lord. The Catholic Church has always offered and still offers to the Sacrament of the Eucharist the cult of adoration, not only during Mass, but also outside of it, reserving the consecrated hosts with the utmost care, exposing them to the solemn veneration of the faithful, and carrying them in procession."

(*Catechism of the Catholic Church*, 1378)

I was confirmed into the Roman Catholic Church on the feast day of St Francis of Assisi, 4th October 2003. Quite early in my new experience as a Roman Catholic, I was asked to consider committing to an hour of Adoration before the Blessed Sacrament, as part of a week-long programme that ran twenty-four hours a day from Monday to Friday in my local parish. I committed to a 2 a.m. to 3 a.m. time slot each Wednesday morning and as of this date, I have been following this schedule for six years.

This book *Praises, Prayers, and Petitions* is a result of my first efforts of trying to focus on themes for prayer before the Blessed Sacrament. I decided to use the letters of the alphabet and create a theme to consider based upon each letter. I committed to twenty-six weeks for this experiment; an hour each week in Adoration in which I would consider a theme and then just write down what thoughts came to me during the session. Before I started each hour, I prayed that the Holy Spirit might guide my thoughts and help me to write them down, in order to learn more about my faith, and to help me learn to love my Lord more.

This booklet contains the unedited thoughts as they came to me while considering each theme. It can be used as a guide for meditation and prayer during one's hour in Adoration before the Blessed Sacrament in several ways.

In the beginning, I would recommend that the Adorer just consider one theme for the session. Read what I have written slowly, and then stop and meditate on each sentence that you have just read. Go back to any specific statement that captured your interest and accept any of your own thoughts that have come to you while considering it and then write them down. You will now be starting to keep a record of your considerations during Adoration.

After some practice at this level, you can begin to just focus on one or two statements within a theme for your hour of Adoration. Try to understand, and expand upon, what that statement, or statements, might mean for you and write it down.

The third way that you can use this book is to just read it quickly through, covering all themes. You will find that you can easily read the whole book within an hour. Again, I would encourage you to try to express in writing any thoughts that come to you in your own words.

I believe that if you have prayed as I have suggested, before each session of Adoration, the Lord will know that you are trying to open yourself to hearing his voice by reading, then considering, then writing, and then by being silent. Prayer can be accomplished through all of these actions.

We have so much to be thankful for, in this opportunity for Adoration of Our Lord in the Most Blessed Sacrament. We place ourselves before Our Lord and Master, awaiting what may come. Some hours might seem unproductive, but we are basking in his sunrays. On other occasions we will gain insights into the themes of our faith that may rival those of the saints that have gone before us.

I invite you to undertake this commitment to Adoration of the Blessed Sacrament within your parish.

Keith Wayne Phillips
13th May 2013
Feast Day of Our Lady of Fatima

ADORATION

"All nations shall come to adore you and glorify your name, O Lord."

Psalm 85:9

∞

All praise to you, Father, Son and Holy Spirit; Three In One. All praise to you Blessed Trinity.

∞

All praise to you, Father, Creator of all that was, all that is, and all that is to come.

∞

All praise to you, Lord Jesus Christ - Our Lord, Our God, and Our Saviour.

∞

All praise to you, Holy Spirit - our guide, our conscience, and our inspiration.

∞

Blessed be the Three In One that have blessed each one of us with a life to be lived in praise and Adoration.

∞

Blessed be our lives to be lived for your glory and for your service - all for you and for others.

∞

Blessed be each moment lived for you, filled with your love, given to others.

Blessed be each opportunity that you place before us to love others and to serve you by serving them.

Blessed be the grace that you give us, unexpected and undeserved, a gift given freely.

Blessed be the strength that you grant us gained through meekness.

Blessed be the hope and promise of an eternal life in your presence; praising and glorifying your name.

Blessed be the love that you give to us in order that we, too, may learn to love.

Blessed be the Church that you have given us - its body, its teachings and its traditions.

Blessed be the Holiness that you have given us as an inspiration through the lives of your saints and servants.

All praise to you, Father, Son, and Holy Spirit - our love, our life and our hope.

BELIEF

"You have been buried with him, when you were baptised; and by baptism, too, you have been raised up with him through your belief in the power of God who raised him from the dead." Colossians 2:12

☙

Help us, O Lord, to know you with and through our minds and our bodies, and all that surrounds us.

☙

Help us, O Lord, and give us the strength to truly believe all that you have taught us through the Church, its prophets, its teachings, and its traditions.

☙

Help us, O Lord, to fully know and understand your words given to us through your Gospels.

☙

Grant us the strength to never doubt and to always hold true to your Way, your Truth, and your Life.

☙

Grant us your grace; for we are weak and cannot live up to your expectations on our own.

☙

Help unbelievers to know you as the one true answer to all of the questions and concerns of life.

∞

Open our minds to all of your great promises, as you have taught us, through your teachings and your parables.

∞

Help all of your children to truly believe in your divine presence in the Blessed Eucharist: Body, Blood, Soul, and Divinity.

∞

Help us, O Lord, to bring others to belief in you through our actions inspired by you, for we can do nothing by ourselves.

∞

Help us, O Lord, to especially bring members of our families back into your fold. Open their hearts and minds to truly believe in you and your promises.

∞

Help us, O Lord, to fully believe in your angels and saints that you have given us as intercessors; that we may truly believe in the help and guidance that they can give us each day.

∞

Help us to truly believe in your promise of an eternal life with you, and help us to never forget this promise as we live each moment of our daily lives.

CALLING

"Who is the author of this deed if not he who calls the generations from the beginning? I, the Lord, who am the first and shall be with the last."

Isaiah 41:4

❧

Help us, O Lord, to discover the true calling and purpose of our lives: to prepare our souls and the souls of others for Eternity.

❧

Help us to listen, O Lord, to your voice as you speak through events and through others each day.

❧

Help us to listen, O Lord, as you speak to us through your inspired words of the Bible.

❧

You call us, O Lord, to Holiness, nothing less. We must be perfect as you, our Father, are perfect.

❧

You have given each soul the ability to hear your voice. If only we would listen to your promptings.

❧

You call us through the marvels of nature to an ordered life in harmony with your intentions.

∞

You call to us through that small inner voice, present within each one of us, to fulfil our purpose in accordance with your plans.

∞

You call some of us to a life with more commitment and more hardship, but all are called to be Holy. Each one of us has a separate and unique journey.

∞

Some are called to the religious life as priests and as nuns, but all are called to be your servants.

∞

You call us to a life of service - serving you by serving others. We must lose all thoughts of ourselves and learn to focus on others.

∞

You call us to love you, Lord, with all of our mind, with all of our strength, with all of our heart, and with all of our soul; you call us to love others as we love ourselves, and as we have been loved by you.

∞

Help us, O Lord, to find our particular calling - the path that you prepared us for.

Deeds

*"But for your part, take courage, do not let your hands
weaken, for your deeds will be rewarded."*

2 Chronicles 15:7

Help us, O Lord, to know that our faith is expressed
through our deeds each day.

If we pray but do not act, we have praised or adored but
we have not demonstrated our love for our Lord who is
present in all.

If we have talked about our love, or have thought about our
love, we still have not shown our love.

Help us to know, O Lord, that you send opportunities to us
each day and you wait to see what we do with each one.

The poor await our assistance; the homeless need our help;
the hungry need a share of our food; will we merely pray
for them?

You have placed these people and their circumstances
within our reach, within our sight; we cannot ignore them.

On the day of judgement you will ask what we have done, not what we have thought about.

∞

Faith must be put into action; this is how we show our love for you: by serving others.

∞

We must demonstrate our love and our compassion for others by addressing and serving their needs. In this way we love and serve you.

∞

Our deeds should be a record of our love for you; a demonstration of our faith in action. The Church has always put its faith into action.

∞

The Church has established hospitals, care facilities, social service agencies, schools, and food-for-the-hungry programmes. It has shown the love of Christ in action by addressing the needs of those around it.

∞

Most of the saints have demonstrated a lifelong commitment to the service of those in need. We must follow their example.

∞

Help us, O Lord, to find the unique way in which you ask each one of us to serve others.

ETERNITY

"...I am your God, I am he from eternity. No one can deliver from my hand, I act and no one can reverse it."

Isaiah 43:12-13

∞

Help us, O Lord, to fully realise that eternity is forever; whether one ends up in heaven or in hell. There will be no end once we are there.

∞

Our purpose on earth is to use the experiences and the people around us to prepare our souls, and the souls of those around us, for eternity with our Father in Heaven.

∞

We must be sanctified, made Holy, before we can ever be ready to exist in the glorious heaven that Jesus has promised is waiting for us.

∞

We can understand this requirement of holiness with our mind; some of us can understand it with our heart; but it is our soul that must truly be ready.

∞

Our time on earth is very limited when we compare it with eternity, or forever. Help us, O Lord, to use each moment that we are given, as if it were an eternity.

∞

We must learn to be ever present in each moment, doing your will; preparing, tempering our souls and those of others, in order that we may be ready for the eternal banquet.

∞

You have called us, O Lord, to an eternal life in your presence and only through your grace granted to us, can we ever hope to be ready, or worthy.

∞

If we are truly present in each moment, especially if we are focused on others, time has no meaning, and that moment becomes an eternity.

∞

Eternal Father, who was, who is, and who will always be, grant us the grace to be ready when our moment of death comes.

∞

Help us, O Lord, to take each moment of life given to us and treat it as though it were an eternal moment. Help us to choose in that moment, to do your will and to let go of self-indulgence.

∞

Now and forever, Amen.

Faith

*"Then he touched their eyes saying, 'Your faith
deserves it, so let this be done for you.'"*

Matthew 9:29

Without faith in God we have nothing: no purpose, no
beginning, no end. We have nothing to live for.

O Lord, you have promised that through faith we can move
mountains; increase our faith.

Faith is a gift from you, Lord; an eternal promise. Help us
to truly believe and not question.

Faith is our mainstay, our rock. In times of trial keep us on
your true path, O Lord.

You have made glorious promises to us; we have no reason
to despair. Help us, O Lord, to increase our faith in what
the Church has taught us; its precepts and its decrees. Let
us never doubt.

You speak through your prophets, your Church, and your
Word. We must truly believe and know that you do not
make false promises.

Faith, Hope and Charity; a gift, a promise and an expectation; all from you, dear Lord.

∞

Our world says that there are many faiths, but there is only one faith, and that is faith in you Lord and your promises.

∞

Help us, O Lord, to unite as one body and one faith. Heal our divisions.

∞

There is one Heaven; a life of eternity united with you Lord. Grant us the grace to always be true to this faith in your promise.

∞

Jesus was "amazed" at the Roman centurion's faith and He said "Never have I found such faith…" (Matthew 8:10) Help us, O Lord, to "amaze" you with our faith.

∞

Jesus admonished Peter for not having the faith to walk on water - "O you of little faith…" (Matthew 14:31) Grant us the grace to "walk on water" in our lives through faith in Him.

∞

Help our mustard seeds of faith to grow into large trees; all for the glory of you, Lord.

GRACE

*"Indeed, from his fullness we have, all of us, received
– yes, grace in return for grace, since, though the Law
was given through Moses, grace and truth have come
through Jesus Christ."*

John 1:16-17

∞

We thank you, O Lord, for the amazing gift of your grace;
without it, we have nothing.

∞

Help us to know, O Lord, that it is your choice to give us
this free and unwarranted gift; we cannot earn it.

∞

Help us to not lose your precious gift, once we have
obtained it.

∞

You have chosen us, Lord, as your adopted sons and
daughters; there can be no greater gift than this.

∞

We struggle on our own for many years and then suddenly
you call us; for reasons only known to yourself.

∞

We cannot know your timing for this precious gift, for some are called to work in your vineyard as a child, and some must wait until their old age.

∞

All of us, Lord, are equal in your eyes once you have called us. you grant us this grace of seeing when we once were blind.

∞

Help us, O Lord, to obtain Holiness in your eyes. We can only do this through the graces that you grant us to overcome our sinful nature.

∞

We cannot win this battle with sin by ourselves. We need your graces to achieve any victory.

∞

Help us, O Lord, to continue to pray for your assistance in this battle with sin, and to be thankful for the many blessings that you have given us in our lives.

∞

You heal us, O Lord, with your touch and your grace. You make us whole and allow us to become one with you when we can never deserve this great privilege.

∞

Thank you Lord; for the gift of your grace.

Holiness

*"May the Lord be generous in increasing your love
and make you love one another and the whole human
race as much as we love you. And may he so confirm
your hearts in holiness that you may be blameless in
the sight of our God and Father when our Lord Jesus
Christ comes with all his saints."*

1 Thessalonians 3:12-13

O Lord, you call each one of us to holiness. All are called
to be saints. Help us on our journey.

∽

Give us the strength to choose to be Holy each moment of
our lives, for it is a choice.

∽

All who are in heaven are Holy and are saints. Therefore
we must consecrate our lives to this goal.

∽

To be Holy is to be consecrated, or set aside, for your
purposes; to worship and glorify your name.

∽

At Baptism, you "marked" us as your adopted sons and
daughters. At Confirmation, you gave us the gift of the
Holy Spirit to guide us on our way to Holiness.

∽

O Lord, we lose our way so easily. Help us to follow your light and not be led off into the darkness.

∞

There are moments of decision each day; help us to choose Holiness rather than separation from you, O Lord.

∞

We become sanctified, or made Holy, through the graces that you bestow upon us. Please help us to become worthy of these graces.

∞

Wash us, O Lord; make us whiter than snow. Cleanse us from our impurities; make us Pure in your eyes.

∞

We thank you, O Lord, for the many examples of Holy saints that you have given us as guides.

∞

Each saint confirms that we are all unique in our journeys and that real progress towards Holiness can be achieved in our daily lives.

∞

The saints achieved Holiness through many challenges; but by perseverance and through your graces, it can be acquired.

∞

O Lord, we all want to be in Heaven someday, and so we all want to achieve Holiness and Sainthood. We must be perfect as you are perfect.

∞

Help us, O Lord, to decide, today, in this moment, to strive for Holiness.

IDOLATRY

"'You shall have no gods except me.'"

Exodus 20:3

∞

O Lord, you commanded us to have no other gods before you, but we fail in so many ways. We worship so many gods.

∞

We worship the god of wealth. Our greed pushes us each day to have, and then to have more. There is no reason for this, as you provide to each one of us what is needed.

∞

Help us, O Lord, to resist this temptation to have so much. You ask us to live simple lives in order that we may discover what is truly important.

∞

We worship the god of fame. We strive to "be somebody" when we already have the greatest gift; we are your children: "a Child of God."

∞

We strive to be the greatest when you have asked us to become the least. Only by doing this will we ever be ready for Heaven.

∞

Help us, O Lord, to become small in order that we may become great in your eyes.

∞

We worship the god of health. We worry about our bodies and continually try to achieve an unattainable perfection defined by those that sell images.

∞

You have asked us to not worry about our bodies as they are temporary. We should worry about our souls which last forever.

∞

Help us, O Lord, to take care of our bodies as though they were a tabernacle for you; but also to accept this marvellous gift that you have given us, and not spend so much time worrying about what others think.

∞

We worship the god of time. We watch it continually, as our lives tick away, but what do we gain?

∞

Can we add or take away moments in our lives? Can we shorten or lengthen a moment? No, our time on earth is a gift from you, O Lord, it is measured out by you, and only has meaning, when we use this gift for your purposes.

∞

Help us, O Lord, to place no other gods before you.

JOY

"But the angel said, 'Do not be afraid. Listen, I bring you news of great joy, a joy to be shared by the whole people. Today in the town of David a saviour has been born to you; he is Christ the Lord."

Luke 2:10-11

∞

O Lord, you sent your only Son to be born of a woman; the greatest event to ever take place in this world, and the angels and shepherds were filled with great joy. What has happened to our joy?

∞

He was sent for all of us; to save our souls and to open the gates of Heaven to the greatest joy that we could ever imagine: to be able to spend eternity with you, O Lord.

∞

O Lord, we have lost our sense of joy for this great event. We have lost our sense of awe and wonder for what you have done for us.

∞

Help us, O Lord, to regain our joy, and to begin again, to spread this news of great joy, to all of the people in our lives.

∞

Help us to bring love, joy and compassion to the elderly, to the poor and to the sick. Let them see the joy of your sweet love in our faces.

Teach us to be like children who express their joy in the simplest things. Help us to regain our sense of wonder in all of your creation.

A simple smile, or a laugh, can drive away all thoughts of despair in the downtrodden. Help us, O Lord, to share this joy of your love with others.

We have been given the greatest gift; a Saviour, a Messiah, was sent to be with us here on earth. What greater joy can there be than this?

O Lord, fill our hearts with joy and then let us share it with others. Lift us up when we feel lost. Help us to focus on you, Lord, and on others, and our joy will return.

Our joy will increase as we let go of our burden of sin. Help us, O Lord, to lay that burden down.

KINDNESS

*"...he himself is kind to the ungrateful and the wicked.
Be compassionate as your Father is compassionate."*
                                                    Luke 6:35-36

∞

Help us, O Lord, to be gentle and considerate in our acts towards others. Teach us to be kind, even to the ungrateful and the wicked, as you are.

∞

Our actions towards one another should be small acts of love; we should be merciful, as you are merciful.

∞

Help us to radiate your love in all that we do and to be considerate to all that we meet.

∞

A simple touch to the hand of the elderly, or a smile from the heart, demonstrates our love for you, O Lord, to others. They can feel your love through our hands; they can see your love in our eyes.

∞

Help us, O Lord, to use these opportunities that you place before us to demonstrate your love through small acts of kindness.

∞

Through these acts of kindness, help us, O Lord, to lead the ungrateful to you. Give us the strength to persevere.

∞

One small act can change the life of another. It can renew lost faith and rekindle hope. Help us, O Lord, to lower our defenses and to open our hearts and allow others to be kind to us as well.

∞

We, too, are ungrateful in so many ways. We often do not accept small acts of mercy that you grant to us each day.

∞

Sometimes your mercy is granted to us through the hands of others. Help us to accept your kindness through the many blessings that you give to us.

∞

The wicked can be changed through loving kindness more easily than through harsh treatment, or avoidance. Give us the strength to continue to love when we meet with resistance.

∞

Thank you, O Lord, for being so loving and kind to us when we are so undeserving. Help us to become more worthy of your graces.

LOVE

*"I give you a new commandment: love one another; just
as I have loved you, you also must love one another."*
                                                    John 13:34.

∞

O Lord, teach us to love others, as you have loved us.
Grant us this grace.
                    ∞

As children we learn what it is to be loved from our parents.
We are vulnerable and must rely on them for everything.
This is how we are to learn to love you: by being loved.

∞

Grant us the grace to accept your love, and then to learn to
love ourselves, and then others.

∞

Love begins with a commitment to another: to always be there
for strength, support and guidance. It must be unconditional.

∞

O Lord, our love for one another is tested in so many ways.
We lose our patience, and then our respect, and then finally
our commitment. It becomes easy to not love anymore.

∞

O Lord, help us to learn to love again as you love us. This process begins by learning to accept love again; to lower our defenses against being hurt by others.

∞

For trial is a part of being loved. It tests our commitment. Open our hearts once again and help us to be as we once were as children.

∞

O Lord, thank you for the great love that you give us. May we learn through your graces how to truly love you, and others.

MERCY

"Happy the merciful: they shall have mercy shown them."
Matthew 5:7

"For judgement will be merciless to one who has shown no mercy; mercy triumphs over judgement"
James 2:13

O Lord, you grant us your mercy each day even though we are so undeserving. Without it we would surely perish.

And yet, we spend a good part of each day judging others and showing no mercy.

Help us, O Lord, to learn from the mercy that you grant us and learn to forgive.

Teach us patience with one another, for in the end you alone will judge our actions.

We should look at ourselves first, and correct our own misdemeanors and sins; for we have such a long way to go to reach the perfection that you demand of us.

Mercy is love in action - unconditional love. Help us, O Lord, to love without judgement.

∞

Thank you, Lord, for your divine mercy. We disappoint you in so many ways, and yet you wait for us to come to you, never forcing, always waiting with open arms, as the prodigal son's father did.

∞

Help us, O Lord, to learn from this example, especially with our families; for they are to be our 'loved ones'.

∞

O Lord, have mercy on us, for we are all sinners.

Need

"Do not be like them. Your Father knows what you need before you ask him."
Matthew 6:8

∞

All that we really need in this life is your love and your graces, O Lord.

∞

You show us your love by granting each one of us what we truly need.

∞

Help us, O Lord, to know the difference between our wants and our needs.

∞

We fill our lives with many material things, trying to satisfy an inner need for love, but your love is all that we need, and you grant it freely, if we but open our hearts.

∞

You satisfy our need for assistance by granting graces. We can do nothing on our own.

∞

You teach us, O Lord, to help others: the poor and the needy. Help us to lead them to you as the one true answer to all of their needs.

∞

If we give the poor material food, but have not shared our love for you, we will not satisfy their hunger.

∞

You teach us, O Lord, to lead a simple life with few needs and yet we fill our lives with so many distractions and then we lose our focus on you.

∞

Help us, O Lord, to simplify our lives - to cut our needs down to the minimal basics. Only then will we regain our love for you.

∞

Help us, O Lord, to share what we have with others who are truly in need. Help us to get rid of the surplus in our lives.

∞

Thank you, Lord, for fulfilling our every real need.

OPENNESS

"Ask, and it will be given to you; search, and you will find; knock, and the door will be opened to you."
Matthew 7:7

∞

Help us, O Lord, to open ourselves to your love, your grace, and your promises.

∞

Open our hearts to your love, for you so loved us that you gave your only begotten son, so that whoever would believe in him would have eternal life.

∞

Help us to learn to love others so that we may love you in return.

∞

Open our lives so that we can accept the many graces that you wish to bestow upon us. Help us to be worthy.

∞

Help us to trust in you wholeheartedly, in faith and in love, so much so, that we open ourselves completely to you.

∞

Open our minds to your promises and keep us from the many distractions that cloud our thoughts and lead us to doubt and despair.

೦೦

Open our eyes so that we might see this wonderful world, and all that it contains, as a sign of your love and your power. Help us to respect this gift.

೦೦

Open our ears so that we may hear you calling to us each day, through the sounds of nature, the voices of the needy and those that love us.

೦೦

Open our arms, so that we may embrace others with your love, proven through our actions.

೦೦

Open our mouths so that we may praise your name, now and forever.

P EACE

"These things I have spoken to you, so that in me you may have peace. In the world you have tribulation, but take courage, I have overcome the world."

John 16:37

∞

"Blessed are the peacemakers, for they shall be called Sons of God"

Matthew 5:8-10

∞

O Lord, we can only have peace in you - there is no other way. Enfold us in your loving arms.

∞

We cannot bring peace without bringing you. Give us the courage to always be a witness to your love.

∞

The world talks of peace, but there is no peace without following your way, your truth and your life.

∞

Our peace is often disturbed through our anger. It is usually a result of our pride. Help us, O Lord, to overcome our failings and to accept your peace within our hearts and souls.

∞

Help us, O Lord, to radiate your peace. Remove all signs of agitation in how we deal with others.

∽

You have asked us, O Lord, to abide in you, and then you will abide in us, and we will have peace.

∽

O Lord, there will be peace in this world for all, when all of the world turns to you.

∽

We thank you, Lord, for the small moments of peace that you grant us as a sign of your promises.

∽

May peace be with us, through you.

QUIETNESS

*"For thus says the Lord God, the Holy One of Israel;
by waiting and by calm you shall be saved, in quiet
and in trust your strength lies."*

Isaiah 30:15

∞

O Lord, we cannot hear you if we surround ourselves with
noise. Help us to appreciate quietness.

∞

Help us to learn to be quiet and to be still - listening for
your voice.

∞

We have lost the art of being still. We fill our days with
busyness, but to what purpose?

∞

Most of our daily moments are wasted - filled with many
mindless deeds, thoughts and words.

∞

Help us, O Lord, to return our focus to you. Once we learn
to do this, all matters will return to their proper place.

∞

We do not need to continually explain ourselves; our actions should speak for themselves.

∞

We feel the need to continually express our opinion, as though it really mattered. All that matters is what you have told us, O Lord, as the Word Made Flesh.

∞

We do not need to be continually busy. We need to learn again how to be still and to "be" quiet.

∞

The hermits of old knew the secret of drawing near to you, O Lord. They learned how to be quiet; they withdrew from a busy world.

∞

Help us, O Lord, to be quiet in the midst of noise - to surround ourselves with your peace.

∞

We thank you, O Lord, for the ability to listen. Give us the grace to be able to hear your voice when others cannot.

Respect

The owner of the vineyard said "What shall I do? I will send my beloved son; perhaps they will respect him."
                                                              Luke 20:13

❦

O Lord, you are the owner of the vineyard and you did send your beloved Son, but we did not respect him then, and we do not respect him now.

❦

We continue to wound you each day with many transgressions, from simple thoughtlessness, to outright cruelty. Forgive us, Lord. ❦

To ask for respect is such a simple thing, much easier than to love, but we fail in so many ways.

❦

We fail to give our respect to the poor, to the aged, to the unborn and yet conceived. We kill through actions, and through inaction. ❦

Teach us, O Lord, to respect all life as a gift from you. Help us to reach out to others and to take a stand.

❦

Help us to truly respect your teachings and expectations, by living our lives as you have commanded. Grant us this grace.

We thank you for the respect that you have given us through the granting of our free will. Help us to use this gift wisely in fulfilling your purposes.

SALVATION

"For God has not destined us for wrath, but for obtaining salvation through our Lord Jesus Christ."
1 Thessalonians 5:9

"There is no other name...by which we must be saved"
Acts 4:12

O Lord, you were sent to save us from ourselves and to show us the one true path to Our Father in Heaven.

You have taught us that we can only be saved through complete surrender to the will of the Father.

We must lose our lives in order to obtain salvation. We must let go of any self-interest and focus on you, Lord, and on others.

We cannot save ourselves; we can only obtain salvation through grace from you, Lord. Help us to be worthy.

Our present lives are nothing compared to the eternal promise that you have given us. Save our souls.

∞

Help us, O Lord, to follow your teachings in order that we might be saved.

∞

The time of salvation is near - help us to live each day as though it were our last.

∞

Thank you, Lord, for the wonderful gift and promise of salvation. Help us to achieve all that you have destined us for.

TRUST

"Blessed is the man who trusts in the Lord and whose trust is the Lord. For he will be like a tree planted by the water, that extends its roots by a stream and will not fear when the heat comes; but its leaves will be green, and it will not be anxious in a year of drought, nor cease to yield fruit."

Jeremiah 17:7-8

⚭

O Lord, you have asked us to place all of our trust in you, and you have promised that all of our true needs will be met.

⚭

The apostles were sent out to teach the gospel and they were to carry no staff, take no money or food, and only rely on the good will of those that they encountered. Their trust was in you Lord, that you would provide.

⚭

Help us, O Lord, to trust in you and to let go of our need to be in control. Grant us this faith.

⚭

Help us to learn to trust one another again, for you work through others, to satisfy our needs.

⚭

Help us, O Lord, to accept our daily struggles as opportunities to demonstrate our trust in you.

∽

We can only bear fruit through trust in you. We can do nothing without your grace.

∽

Help us to surrender to your love and your graces.

UNITY

"Just as a human body, though it is made up of many parts, is a single unit because all these parts, though many, make one body, so it is with Christ."

1 Corinthians 12:12

∽

Help us, O Lord, to be perfected in unity. Heal our divisions.

∽

O Lord, you established one church with you as its head and we are to be its body; each one of us as an integral part of the whole.

∽

And yet we have created divisions. For power, or pride, we have created separation when we were to be united as one body through faith in you.

∽

Your church has become a matter of names and buildings and famous leaders rather that humble servants of you, Lord.

∽

Help us, O Lord, to become united again within you, and you within us, as one body, one church - for your glory, not ours.

∽

Help us, O Lord, to spread your word, so that all in the world may know of your love for us, and may come to believe in your Way, your Truth, and your Life.

∽

You, Lord, are the one true answer to all that concerns us in this life, and in the next eternal life. Help us to be one flock under one shepherd.

Vanity

"But I said, "I have toiled in vain, I have spent my strength for nothing and vanity; yet surely the justice due to me is with the Lord, and my God" Isaiah 49:4

∞

O Lord, we have wasted so much time. We spend our lives in a vain attempt to better ourselves, and yet we cannot, without your help and your graces.

∞

We are taught to believe in so many things, and yet we lose our belief in you, as if it were of little importance.

∞

You have given us two great commandments, and all that we do should reflect our pursuit and achievement of these two tasks. All else is vanity and self-indulgence. Help us, O Lord, to let go of this focus on self and grant us the grace to focus on you and on others.

∞

All that we do should reflect our love for you, Lord, and for others; our reward will be granted through your graces - eternal life with you. ∞

Self-indulgence separates us from you, Lord. Heal us from ourselves. ∞

We thank you, Lord for this precious gift of life. Help us to use each moment for your purposes, and not our own.

WORLDLINESS

"For what will it profit a man if he gains the whole world and forfeits his soul?"

Matthew 16:26

O Lord, our task in this life is to prepare our souls, and those of others, for eternity, and yet we get distracted by so many worldly things.

We need to ask ourselves, "Does this activity bring me closer to you, Lord, or will it cause separation?"

We need to ask ourselves, "Will this item for purchase aid me in my journey to eternal life, or is it a burden?"

Our lives are meant to be simple, not complicated - through trust in you, not in this world.

You have given us many natural wonders in this world; your grace is sufficient, and yet we try to create our own world.

Help us, O Lord, to realise that a world that we create is not your world; we have no power or authority.

Teach us to use the gifts that you have given us in this world for your purposes, according to your plan.

∞

We thank you for this world as a place to practice and learn what is necessary in order to return to you in eternal life.

X=CHRIST

X represents the Greek letter chi (=ch), the first letter of *Christos* (the Greek word for Christ).

∞

"And you also were included in Christ when you heard the word of truth, the gospel of your salvation. Having believed, you were marked in him with a seal; the promised Holy Spirit."

Ephesians 1:13

∞

"Baptism seals the Christian with an indelible spiritual mark (character) of his belonging to Christ. No sin can erase this mark, even if sin prevents Baptism from bearing the fruits of salvation."

Catechism of the Catholic Church, Article 1272

∞

In the days of old, if a man couldn't write his signature, he would make his "mark", and that mark was an X.

∞

We are asked to make our mark in life. Our mark should be the mark of Christ.

∞

O Lord, you have marked us as your own through Baptism; help us to fulfil the destiny that you have chosen for us.

∞

The evil one can see that we are marked, and that we are yours; help us to resist his temptations.

∞

Give us the grace to proudly wear the mark that you have placed upon us Lord. We thank you for claiming us as your own.

YEARNING

*"O God, you are my God: I shall seek you earnestly;
my soul thirsts for you, my flesh yearns for you, in a
dry and weary land where there is no water"*

Psalm 63:1

O Lord, we need you; we yearn for you. There is no one
else that can satisfy our hunger.

The path towards salvation has many trials and tribulations
on the way. Our innate need for you drives us onward.

You satisfy our every need; we yearn to be filled with your
love and your graces.

Help us, O Lord, when we become lost and weary; quench
our thirst for you.

We long to be united with you, Lord, for all eternity. Guide
us on our way.

Our yearning is our need for your love. We know in our
hearts that you love each one of us.

O Lord, give us the strength to continue to progress in our love for you, and for others.

∞

We shall seek you earnestly all the days of our lives, until that day, when through your graces, we will be united with you.

ZEAL

"Then his disciples remembered the words of scripture: Zeal for your house will devour me."

John 2:17

Our lives should be driven by our love for you, Lord; fill us with passion.

Let us be a witness in every way to your teachings and your love.

Give us the strength and courage to persist, when all of the world seems to be against us. Fill us with zeal.

Help us to fight, O Lord, for what is just and compassionate as we deal with those that we encounter each day.

Help us, O Lord, to find others that will join us in this battle to win souls; for we have strength in numbers with your grace.

Help us to proclaim your word with strength and conviction.

Let us be true soldiers in your army of salvation, setting the captives free.

⁓

We know that no harm can come to us with you by our side.

⁓

We thank you, Lord, for the zeal that you have planted within us. Help us to live each moment of our lives filled with thoughts of eternity with you. Amen.